For the Sleepwalkers

FOR THE SLEEPWALKERS

Poems by Edward Hirsch

Alfred A. Knopf   New York   1981

THIS IS A BORZOI BOOK
PUBLISHED BY ALFRED A. KNOPF, INC.

Grateful acknowledgment is made to the editors of the
following publications where these poems first appeared:
"Dusk," "Prelude to Spring," "Impressions: Monet," and
"Regret" were originally published in *The New Yorker*.
"Factories" first appeared in *Partisan Review*, Spring, 1980.
"How to Get Back to Chester" and "For the Sleepwalkers"
were first published in *Poetry*.

Other poems in this book have been previously published in
*Agni Review, Antioch Review, Beloit Poetry Journal, Black
Warrior Review, Boundary 2, Carleton Miscellany, Concerning
Poetry, Denver Quarterly, Footprint Magazine, Garcia Lorca
Review, Georgia Review, Iowa Review, Kansas Quarterly,
The New Republic, Paris Review, Poetry Northwest, Poetry
Now, The Sewanee Review, Skywriting, Southern Review,
The Times Literary Supplement* (London), and *Yale Review*.

Grateful acknowledgment is made to Harper & Row, Publishers,
Inc., for permission to reprint a line from *Collected Poems* by
Arthur Rimbaud, Copyright © 1967, 1970, 1971, 1972, 1975
by Paul Schmidt; and to Viking Penguin, Inc., for permission to
reprint a line from "Love in America?" from *The Complete
Poems of Marianne Moore*, Copyright © 1966 by
Marianne Moore.

Special thanks to the Thomas J. Watson Foundation, the
Amy Lowell Foundation, and the Ingram Merrill Foundation
for their support during the writing of this book.

"Dance You Monster to My Soft Song!" takes its title from a
painting by Paul Klee.

Library of Congress Cataloging in Publication Data
Hirsch, Edward.
    For the sleepwalkers.
    I. Title.
PS3558.I64F6   811'.54   80-2726
ISBN 0-394-51474-2
ISBN 0-394-74908-1 (pbk.)

Manufactured in the United States of America

FIRST EDITION

for Janet

CONTENTS

I

Song Against Natural Selection   3
Apologia for Buzzards   4
Dusk   5
Poets, Children, Soldiers   6
"Dance You Monster to My Soft Song!"   7
A Valentine from Rimbaud   8
Insomnia   10
Cocks   11

II

How to Get Back to Chester   21
Gérard de Nerval: Fairy Tale for a Whore   22
At the Grave of Marianne Moore   24
The Sweatshop Poem   25
At Kresge's Diner in Stonefalls, Arkansas   26
Garbage   28
Reminiscence of Carousels and Civil War   30
Christopher Smart   32
For the Sleepwalkers   34

III

Prelude to Spring   37
With Isaac Babel in Odessa   38
Interlude During War: Paul Klee   39
Still Life: An Argument   40
Matisse   42
The Enigma: Rilke   44
Equinox   46
Regret   47
Dance of the Moon   48
A Walk with Vallejo in Paris   50

IV

Little Political Poem   55
Factories   56
A Letter   57
Walking the Upper West Side, with Lorca   58
A True Account of the Fabulous Ascent of a Unicorn with
    a Retarded Girl in New York City Last Night   60
Denial   63
Nightsong: Ferris Wheel by the Sea   64
The Acrobat   66
Song   70

V

Sonata   73
A Chinese Vase   74
Impressions: Monet   76
The River Merchant: A Letter Home   78
And So It Begins Again   79
The Dark Sun
    I.   Proem: Early Morning   80
    II.   Parable of Wyverns   81
    III.   Cantata for a Dutch Elm   82
    IV.   Dusk: Elegy for the Dark Sun   83
Transfigured Night, Come Down to Me, Slowly   84

I

SONG AGAINST
NATURAL SELECTION

The weak survive!
A man with a damaged arm,
a house missing a single brick, one step
torn away from the other steps
the way I was once torn away
from you; this hurts us, it

isn't what we'd imagined, what
we'd hoped for when we were young
and still hoping for, still imagining things,
but we manage, we survive. Sure,
losing is hard work, one limb severed
at a time makes it that much harder

to get around the city, another word
dropped from our vocabularies
and the remaining words are that much heavier
on our tongues, that much further
from ourselves, and yet people
go on talking, speech survives.

It isn't easy giving up limbs,
trying to manage with that much
less to eat each week, that much more
money we know we'll never make,
things we not only can't buy, but
can't afford to look at in the stores;

this hurts us, and yet we manage, we survive
so that losing itself becomes a kind
of song, our song, our only witness
to the way we die, one day at a time;
a leg severed, a word buried; this
is how we recognize ourselves, and why.

Nobody welcomes me, nobody. And yet
the sun that beats through the ribs of the sky
beats with a heavy pulse, like the heart,
hollowing out the skull and spoiling the flesh,
tattooing the ground, flaming with a heat
that turns oceans of blood into quarries
of bone, and makes even the cactus writhe.
But nobody despises the sun, nobody.

The sky, too, is a map of quarries
and caves, parched like a canvas, and
wrinkled from the blear-eyed motion
of a sparse wind. A violent muscle is
pumping blood through a few scattered clouds
until a violent color sizzles up in the ground.
I, too, have a heart and wings, and I
say that a single pulse animates the world.

I ask nothing more than the sun:
to be hoisted up like a flag into the
early morning, and left suspended in the sky;
to be worked under like heat, to be
honored for light, and to be escorted
carefully through the dry tedium of day
until, hungry and hesitant at dusk,
plunging into a wilderness of colors.

The sun is going down tonight
like a wounded stag staggering through the brush
with an enormous spike in its heart
and a single moan in its lungs. There

is a light the color of tarnished metal
galloping at its side, and fresh blood
is steaming through its throat. Listen!
The waves, too, sound like the plunging

of hooves, or a wild hart simply
crumpling on the ground. I imagine
there are hunters beating through the woods
with their scythes and their tired dogs

chasing the wounded scent, and I suppose
there are mothers crying out for their children
in the fog. Because it is dusk. Yes,
dusk with its desperate colors of erasure,

its secrets of renunciation, and its long
nightmares beyond. And now here is the night
with its false promise of sleep, its wind
leafing through the grass, its vacant

spaces between stars, its endless memory
of a world going down like a stag.

Soiled thoughts and poor weapons,
tonight I am too exhausted to prepare
for the old wars with sleep,

the nightly struggle between the sofa
and the bedroom, the distinguished window
and the iron stair. I'm tired

of living like a broken yellow oar
awash in the blue waters of nightfall,
or a homesick soldier who never left

home for the war. Poets and children
and soldiers know about the black
trenches of moonlight on the ceiling,

the shadows that leave no traces
of water on the floor. Dead seagulls
hover like headlights in the corners

and the darkest mirror extends inwards
for at least a thousand years. Believe me,
there are no fairy tales of insomnia,

no escapes from the thumbprint of darkness,
and yet in the sickly half-light of morning
I imagine us coming out into the streets,

poets and children and soldiers, all,
all of us together, all of us swaddled
with real bodies, with strange human bodies,

all of us wrapped in the slender tinsel
of our wars and our deep secrets,
all of us weighted down by our moons

and our dead planets, all of us
spinning out into the day together.

Tonight it begins with the mystery
Of a tired shopgirl crawling out of her kitchen window
To watch the first fires of dusk on the river,
The stunned stars lighting up like leaves,
And the sky smouldering with the pink smoke
Of early winter. There's a slow barge
Breaking a stone tunnel through the waves
And, for a moment, she thinks of a few trees
Already undressed, opening their arms
To the water, and she begins to shudder
As if she, too, had stepped out of her leaves,
Stepped out of her dress into the evening. But
The sky is close and warm; the light is
A blue scarf wrapped around her neck,
And the shadows form a soft blanket under her.
The fire escape arches its back like a bridge
Or descends into the streets like a ladder
And because the window is still standing open
Behind her, there are no regrets,
There are so many memories of daylight
Although for a moment she almost forgets
Herself and steps out into the air forever
Almost dancing, almost afraid to dance, almost
Afraid of whispering a soft song and
Letting it begin once more with the mystery
Of dusk settling on the river like a
Yellow crown, or like a black fire, or like a
Tired shopgirl crawling out of her kitchen window
To watch the sky flaming to a momentary stillness
And bearing a slow dusk dragged slowly
Across the river like a barge breaking a
Stone tunnel through the waves. And afraid
To hear the city promising her
This stillness, this secret; promising this,
And that much more in the night to come.

"Our desires still lack a cunning music."

Already I'm sick of this filthy light
Assassinating the branches, exposing the storefronts
With their floor shows of models: women
With flat feet and fluttery hands
Flaunting their asses, while their men—
Sad props for elegant lounge coats—
Are attached to the floor behind them.
Poor niggers. I swear if it weren't
For the red letters lighting the glass
I wouldn't know the dummies
Inside from the dummies out here
Since our bodies, too, are plastic.

It's dawn. And the only animals left
On the streets are the stray pigs chasing
The dogs: women with used-up breasts and
Drunks with hands grown into their pockets
Like roots that have turned back. So:
Let's lop off their wrists and leave
The stumps drooping from their sleeves
Like flags over a bridge. And when
That's all through let's carve up
Our own ankles. Because I'm sick of
Walking around upright, and besides
How else can we cure those strange creatures

Who keep saying "Dear," and "Dearest,"
And "Thank you so much for the wine," and
"Please pass the salt and pepper."
Shit! Sweetheart, from now on
Let's multiply like vermin and then
Crawl quietly into the canal
With dead worms breeding in our organs
And the ugliest houseflies hanging
From our lips. I'll drown you.
You'll strangle me. And somehow we'll
Manage to pass, decently into

A decent oblivion.

Undressing the cold body
you lie down at dusk, blue shine

on the windows and the sun
husked for winter night. Tight-lipped

and longing to embody sleep,
to devour the white lion

sleep, you watch the room slowly
steep itself in shadows, steep

itself in the wine-flushed darkness
of another night. Silently

you confront the blue-rimmed edge
of outer dark, those crossroads

where we meet the dead, knowing
their first street calls will rise

and nuzzle against your chest
like tiny inexorable animals

or the blunt edge of a knife
about to descend. And all night

you're left sitting at a desk
frightened, thinking of the skull

under the smooth skin, how we
return to our lives as animals

engulfed in soft fog, exposed
to the wind against our fur

and denied warmth, denied rest,
denied earth's sleep and granite.

COCKS

I.

Look for a red mist rising out of the bare hills
Like the last velvet smoking jacket
Of the Archduke going up, well, in a cloud
Of plush smoke fogging over a small lake
In the country. I mean the first image

Of nostalgia should be as fat and drowsy
As pears ripening in the rich dew of early morning
In a little village just beyond Bougival.
Surrounded by fields of barley and rye, and
Warmed by a warm sun buried in a vault

Of pear trees, and a thick Moroccan carpet
Of purple clouds. Think of châteaus and country
Manors with kitchen gardens. With carriage houses
And racing stables. With stiff iron cocks
Flapping, like church bells, on all the rafters,

And feathers and claws in all the barns.
The cock says Cocteau twice, and lives on his own farm.
Long live the cock! And long live the cock's crow,
Crowed twice, of the cock's song. Sung twice.
Of the splendid cruelty of the cock

Clawing the nostalgias. Clawed, yes, twice.
Once, as a child, I drew a watercolor
Of the watery lights of our summer house
Shining through a dense fog in the distance.
There was a kitchen garden inked in yellow

And speckled like, well, like a velvet smoking jacket
Going up in fog; and I remember a bruised sun
Buried in a lair of purple clouds. Perhaps that sun
Was the round, balding head of an Algerian cabbage
Hiding from the eyes of a French hunting rabbit,

Or the fleshy green skull of a pumpkin
Brushed with oranges and only the brightest golds.
You must always remember this: *There are
Poets and grown-ups*. Sighs and sobs. Songs
And secrets. But inside every grown-up

There's a live pumpkin pursing its thick lips
To carry the servants to the ball, and the children
To Sunday Mass; to the High Mass of going
To High Mass; Sunday's promise of dazed suns
And sundaes. There is no such thing as a grown-up!

And always we would wake to the sound
Of salt bacon sizzling in the kitchen
And to the cry of cocks calling us to the window
To watch the gatekeeper leading the stallions
From the stable, and to search for grandfather

Striding through the pear trees, and yes,
To point to the tear-stained faces of pumpkins
Bristling with worms in the open field.
Even then the cock crowed twice in the mist
Like a real poet, singing in the splendid plumage

Of a lounge coat. And what did he sing?
My friend: Look for a red mist rising
Out of the bare hills like the last velvet
Smoking jacket of nostalgia going up in a
Cloud of thick smoke; in the smoke of clouds.

You must always remember this:
There were real poets in those days; there
Were cocks cocked upwards on all the chimneys;
There were pumpkins carved inside the grown-ups;
There were worms bristling inside the pumpkins!

II. 1917

> "Next he is talking about a woman at Red Cross
> headquarters who shouted on the staircase.
> 'I was promised fifty wounded men this morning.
> I want my fifty wounded men.'"
>
> —André Gide

Look for the spangled scar of a crayfish
Crawling backwards, always crawling backwards

Over the veined map and dried parchment
Of Apollinaire's shaved head. See how it

Creeps out of the pale blue chapel of his skin
Into the deep trenches and dry riverbeds

Curving all the way from the occupied bank
Of his damaged ear to the eastern front

Of his forehead. Settling into his skull
Like a deep soot, or a heavy liquid dust.

An oily red scar craving a death wound!
A salted claw clawing a parchment of flesh!

And still the words are amethysts and rare
Moonstones watering out of his watery

Blue lips. Understand what I'm saying:
The poems live! And the crayfish. And the war

Has a salt and pepper beard, like Proust;
And sits in a wicker chair, like Stravinsky;

And whimpers with the dry voice
Of a dog dreaming in a dreamless trench.

Picasso has solved the problem of the window hasp!
I have solved the problem of the beatific

Vision of beasts entombing the fables
Of beauty. And Apollinaire has solved

The problem of the crayfish waiting
In every poet's lungs. Crawling in and out

Of doors and windows. Grasping through mirrors.
Pumping blood to the furthest arteries, like a heart.

Spilling water and sand and seaweed on the sidewalks.
Singing!

But look at it this way: The guardian
Angel of poetry sits in a wicker chair.

And dribbles milk down a salt and pepper beard.
And howls with the raw voice of a warrior

Ceaselessly trying to astonish us;
To astonish, yes, and to offend.

III. Pagodas

Look for a sulphur-crested cockatoo
Squatting, like an epaulet, on my shoulder
As I step into a small boat on a dusty
River at dusk with an ageless woman
Perhaps a geisha, perhaps instead a widow
Stepping out of her dry kimono into the night.

Showing two small almonds hardening in the cold.
A crescent moon, shaped like a scar, carved
Across her neck. And a fistful of faded
Plum blossoms. We touch. A wind cracks up
Against the boat, against the taut wood
Of our skins. Or think of it

This way: for us,
Under the enormous branches of the night's
First stars, there is only the smoky
Body of heat smoking in the bodiless cold,
The unbearable liquids of dusk, the steam
Steaming from another river's source.

Later, we begin rowing.
Rowing and rowing into the shadows
Of giant poplars folded over the water
Like carpets. Hovering over the dark edges like
Dragons. Arching into the sky like enormous bridges.
Breathing in and out the mysterious silence, the stillness.

There's a rustle of shoulders shouldering the wind.
There's a sound of oars slapping against the waves.
And suddenly, there's the voice of an old woman
Speaking about her life; this terrible sadness,
Her stained hands, her lost kimonos, the
Rows and rows of empty pagodas

Shining through a dense fog in the distance.
And finally, the weight of holding up
So many nights, so many other winds, so
Many blank tunnels running all the way
From her thin shoulders to her tired head
Is too much for her, and she begins

To nod, dozing off, rowing
Into the thick branches of fog
Until the soft movement of the oars
Becomes the sound of her heavy breathing.
All of her dreams now are of morning; and suddenly
The cockatoo begins singing of life

On another planet in another century, say,
In Paris in the Thirties. Paris? in the Thirties?
Try to think of a strange, uninhabitable country
Where all the people are citizens, yes,
With backaches and jobs. Songs and secrets.
Sobs and sighs. Sorrows. Silences.

There is no such thing as a cockatoo!
No such thing as a cock's crow, crowed twice
On a cock's farm. No such thing as a
Drowsy woman stepping off a wet pier
Into an empty boat. Opening her dry lungs
To the dust. Rowing out into the tides, naked!

My friend: *Life is a horizontal fall,*
Falling. And I admit to having lied, lying down.
And standing up. But always smoking the poppy,
The patient flower. And still the giant elms
Cast dragon shadows on the Seine; the pagodas
Shine through the clouds in the distance.

I am a lie that always tells the truth!
And sometimes the truth is a small man
With a reed pipe and a desperately thin face
Wandering through an empty castle
Of thoughts and dried skins,
Rising out of the thick smoke of the past and future.

You can look for me in the mist of that castle
Keeping the poppy's vigil of rowing,
The woman's vigil of sadness, the cock's song.

IV. Saint-Blaise-des-Simples
    I remain with you.

There's the sight of me
Dressed crudely as the ghost of Orpheus
Searching through the rags and scum of the streets
For a drunken bum sleeping peacefully
Under the dust and torn threads of an old
Fisherman's net. I sing; I
Dance on a nest of water to find him!
Why? Because this bum is not a bum
But a tiny chapel with a moat and a walled garden,
And a ceiling carved with my own offending angels,
Yes, and a voice that says: *Submit;*
You must submit! So enter and submit.
And stoop for me, please, in the entranceway.
Think of me in the moat outside
Still singing. Search for me in the tailpiece
Star scalded in the furthest corners,
Into the murals of beasts and fanatic angels.
Look for me in the wistful eyes
Of a cat staring up at the terrible ghost
Of Orpheus. It's me! Yes, it's me.
So cock your ear to the ground, and listen
To the sound of the deepest waters, the wind
Steaming out of the dirt, the dead cocks
Singing of all that is warm and near,
The earth, the new day,
The inconsolable burden that is ours.

II

HOW TO GET BACK
TO CHESTER

I remember the greasy moon floating
like a tire over the highway, the last
stars flecked like dust on the window
of my father's garage. For years I've walked
away from the concrete fields of a lousy
childhood, the damp haze of life in Chester,

but now I've come back to follow the
moon through the toothed stacks of chimneys,
through the back alleys lit up by shabby
yellow lanterns. I've come here to stand
like a pilgrim before the tin shacks
holding their tin ears on the highway

while trucks roar by without stopping
and factories clack their fat tongues
together in wind. I've come here to listen
to strangers talk about football, to waitresses
talk about strangers. I've come to see myself
taking the deep blasts from an old furnace.

Not much has changed here, and yet
not much is left of childhood, either.
If you want to get back to Chester
you have to listen; you have to stand
like a penitent in your bare feet
and feel the air darken before a storm;

you have to stare at the one viny
plant waving on the family porch
until you feel your father's grimy palm
gripping your hand, until you finally taste
the words at the back of your own mouth, saying
Don't come back, son. And welcome.

GÉRARD DE NERVAL:
FAIRY TALE FOR A WHORE

Nerval, I say to myself, quiet down,
Calm yourself. It's bad enough that the Prince
Of Nerva is nervous, and the Duke of Nerva,
And the Duke's German shepherd, Prince,
And the Princess's French pekapoo, Duke.
It's bad enough that the Duke and the
Prince are barking together in the dark

While the hoot owls in the haunted wood
Hoot back at the loud castle, loudly
Repeating the dogs by repeating themselves.
It's bad enough that you're standing on
The floor of the roof of this fairy palace
Feeling ridiculous, looking down nervously
At Nerva's deftly veiled window, and wondering

If the Princess is concealed somewhere inside,
Say behind the shades, or in the thick velvet
Curtains; wondering if the Prince can hear
The French Duke, or the Duke the German Prince.
Maybe they're watching her undress in the corner!
Because you know she's in there, whispering
Some soft watery secret to the Prince

As she lifts her velvet skirt for the Duke.
Or else you can almost, you can almost hear her
Whispering some damp family secret to the Duke
As she lifts her damp skirt for the Prince
Moaning softly. Where *is* the Duchess anyway?
Gogol would understand this. So would Faust.
And so would the old man who washes the statue

Of the Virgin in the vestibule of the church.
If only those damned Russian hoot owls would
Just stop hooting so that I could hear her!
If only the Prince would stop whispering
Nervously to the Duke while the Duke looks
Wildly around the room for the Duchess.
If only the Duke and the Prince outside

Would stop quarreling about the darkness
In the garden and the light on the cold roof.
Would anyone understand this ideal love? Would I?
If only I could forget the claws in my pockets,
The lobster clawing at my legs. If only I
Could live in the world instead of next to it!
This is how it always ends, happily ever after:

With the Prince and the Duke prying open the
Princess's legs with their fingers, like a knife;
With the Duke and the Prince spreading the Princess's
Thighs on the mattress, like soft butter. How do I
Know this? I know by fairy tales of erotic love,
By the way the dogs paw at the ground, by the way
The wild owls mate with voices in the wind.

AT THE GRAVE OF
MARIANNE MOORE

"Whatever it is, let it be without affectation."

Here lies a lady who knew
that orangutans in the zoo
are still orangutans, that llamas in a caged
park, pecking their llaman food (unpropped and unstaged)
for an unruly foreign audience
throwing bad peanuts, have the common sense

to go about their daily business
unconcerned, intent, though not intent
on their performance, agile without clumsiness,
graceful in the graceful knowledge of their own strength;
who admired a stork's scrupulous skill
in avoiding a belligerent reptile

who was haunted by his own bars
and roared with imprecision
at the stork, and at the constellations of stars.
This was a woman who paid dazzling attention
to all the minor nuances of motion;
the bobbing heads of birds, the strict tension

of snakes slithering through the weeds,
the marvelous quickness of badgers
who raced through their cages like perfect athletes,
almost as artful as her beloved Dodgers.
She saw animals as metaphors for art,
but loved them for their own sake, their own dark

and unpardonable beauty.
Under this ground lies a lady
who had a sense of language that was as wild
as an animal, but who measured depth by silence
or restraint, and whose scrupulous method
in verse bequeathed us a heritage,

the honesty of her intelligence.

There are thirty-one shallow graves in August
with thirty-one swollen coffins, waiting.

During the day I work in a sweatshop
sewing the pink slips and cotton dresses,
the cashmere skirts and thick tweeds
of winter. During the day my fingers
hum with needles, the needles slide
through patches of steaming cloth.
I am preparing the hottest iron.
I am preparing the warmest clothes
for the beautiful thighs of young models
and the sweating hips of new mannequins.
All day I am prepared for leaving.

And at night the factory is silent.
My tired face dims in the window, my
shadow paces through the empty corridors,
alone. At night the cloth in my hands
never whispers with other men's dreams
or purrs with other women's secrets.
My exhausted body is too heavy for clothes.
All night the heavy tongue of summer repeats
its one heavy syllable, its one drooling
syllable of stupor; the crystal glass
of another night asks me to drink.
And I do drink, deeply.
And later I lie in the naked sheets
without sleeping, without breaking the door
or plunging into the river. Without screaming.

But sometimes I move through the house, slowly.
Sometimes I sit in the dark kitchen
or stand at the swollen bathroom window
to watch the glistening blue worm,
the invisible needle of moonlight
sewing a dark shroud for my body.

AT KRESGE'S DINER
IN STONEFALLS, ARKANSAS

Every night, another customer.
One night it's a state trooper,
the next a truck driver going all the way
to Arlington, Georgia. Tonight
it's only a tourist, a northerner.
I prefer the truck driver.

You can trust a truck driver.
Tourists are effeminate, though good customers.
I hate it most on Thursday night
when that hog who wants me to go all the way
with him comes in; some state trooper!
I'd rather go to bed with a pig, a northerner!

Well, maybe not a northerner.
They do have peculiar ways.
Still, they're good customers.
I think I hate that fat trooper
as much as I hope my truck driver
comes back on Thursday night.

Only three more nights!
How long does it take a good driver—
'course he doesn't have a Buick like the trooper
or a sports car like that northerner—
to cross Georgia? If I didn't have a customer
I'd go all the way

to Georgia after him, all the way!
I bet I could send a message with that northerner.
You know truckers are the safest drivers.
He's not only my favorite customer
but I dream about him at night.
Maybe I could send a telegram with that trooper

but then I hate asking the trooper
for favors 'cause he wants favors on Thursday night.
Still, I wish he was here instead of that northerner.
You can make a life with a truck driver.
I wonder if he would ever take me away
with him. I wish he was my husband instead of my customer!

O maybe this Thursday night that truck driver, my favorite
    customer,
will push aside the trooper and flick ashes at the northerner,
o and maybe he will take me away.

Work drives you like wind
between suburban houses, emptying cans.
You are invisible as air
and as necessary, more efficient
than a flood leveling cities,
sweeping across plains; this city
can't survive without you.
Its houses are a body
releasing fluids, endlessly
emptying and filling with breath,
cleansing blood. Its refuse
is your job, and you
are devoted to it
like a disease, or the icon
of an obscure god.
Waste is your fool's gold.
And so you trek across lawns,
sweeping through alleys, relaxing
on your way back to the dump.
How much you would despise company!
For centuries you have been working alone.
On the patio you are silent
as fog, an atmosphere so regular
that even the family dogs
conspire to ignore you.
Sometimes through the glass
you see a husband throwing
his arms up in despair, or a wife
stumbling into a closet.
Once you watched as a woman
unbuttoned her housecoat
in the kitchen, and laid down
on the cold floor; and you knew
then that you would never quit,
anxious and lonely, wounded for good.

She moved away many years ago
though at night you still
remember the dry sheen
of her body, reflected against tile
like the sun on a plastic cup.
And during the day you dream
of opening the door, listening for
the sound of children in the window
or the tumble of footsteps
on the stair. She doesn't hear you
entering, and looking down
at her composed body, you sense
strange violence, the light
throbbing in your skull, the rich
tumult of fluids inside you.

REMINISCENCE OF CAROUSELS
AND CIVIL WAR

How two black boys stepping out of a carousel in the park
Resemble a spotted horse working its way
Out of a cold lake in the rain. And how

A spotted horse shaking the water from its mane
Resembles two young country girls dancing
On a makeshift wooden stage at a county fair

In rural Georgia. And how those two young girls
Move with the special grace of Nigerian clowns,
Say, aging transvestites, or two ashen milk trees

Clacking in a hard wind. It's raining. There
Are white fluids seeping from the roots and leaves
And the wind moves through the watery branches

With the muffled sound of horses crossing a lake
With soldiers under the cover of nightfall,
Or two girls pattering barefoot across a stage.

There is blood and real milk rising in the fields
And the oats are mixed with alfalfa and rye.
The scarecrows are down, and the cornfields,

Like the cows and the thin young girls,
Are barren. And those two barren girls dancing
Together on a stage are really only daughters,

My daughters, and those two young boys
Are really slaves. Not that it matters.
What matters is this: Tonight at the fair

I remembered that sometimes the blood pours
From a man's body like the crowds spilling out
Of a circus tent on a Sunday evening in the summer.

This is farfetched, I know, but my brother
Was shot in the chest seven times and
It took him seven hours to bleed to death.

Dead, he still dines. This has been going on
For years, but never has he watched me watching him!
We come after. We *do* come after. And still

The girls move like puppets across the stage.
The acrobats tumble out of their artificial skies.
And the clowns turn somersaults in lavender blouses.

But think of it this way: After a war
The dead and the living move back into the shadows
Like two dazed boys stepping out of a carousel

And then wandering off into the trees in the park,
Or two white country girls unzipping their party dresses.
Are they sisters or daughters? It's dark.

One of the girls touches the other on the wrist.
Suddenly her skin glistens like a horse's neck.
Her breasts are small and her nipples are hard.

There are some things I would rather just forget!
But sometimes at night I begin to shout in my sleep.
The puppets dance. And it's true, it's uncanny

How a man with a chest full of orange blood
Can resemble a clown dressed in a lavender blouse.
And how two young girls stepping off a stage

Can resemble two brothers folding into each other's arms.
And how the country roads look like carousels flattened!
And how the cannons explode in the air like real cannons!

"For they work me with their harping irons,
which is a barbarous instrument, because
I am more unguarded than others."

I am a wild ass galloping through the streets
Trailing the dog star, the mad gull. I am
A white raven spilling light through the skies
Like a colorful beacon, trailing the wild ass,
The laden bull. I am the hooves and the wings

Of the mule clattering through the streets
On a wild journey to Bedlam, a journey
Into a desert of pocked houses and
A whirlpool of dead trees, dead cactus. There
Are buzzards shuddering in the vacant branches.
There is a holy ram swallowing its tongue
At the mirage of a water hole. There is
A calf inside the ram inside the bull
Swallowing its own blood. And I am kneeling

Under the calf's small belly in the street.
It's snowing. The moon is taking off her garments
Like an unruly queen; the desert prophet
Has swallowed his tongue. There are
Lizards crawling through the snow in the
Footprints of the goose, the wild ram.
The bull is weeping. And mother,

I am naked now; I am wondrous nude.
And it is still snowing. I am underneath
The knife constantly, chained at the ankles,
Squirming in my slaughtered ram's body. I am
Racing through the pocked streets under the
Moon's wild eye. The winds are howling.
The clouds are peeling away like the skin
Of a dead man's body. I am fleeing

Into the desert on a wild ass
Trailing a dog star. And believe me,
The ass is dead. Its body is hardening
Between my wild legs hardening in the cold.
The buzzards are riding out into the blizzard
To move the blood, and to moor the corpse. Because
The night is fierce; the desert winds are
Scraping along the ground. The moon is flecked
With the blood of hooves. And it's snowing.
It is always snowing in the country of the mad.

Tonight I want to say something wonderful
for the sleepwalkers who have so much faith
in their legs, so much faith in the invisible

arrow carved into the carpet, the worn path
that leads to the stairs instead of the window,
the gaping doorway instead of the seamless mirror.

I love the way that sleepwalkers are willing
to step out of their bodies into the night,
to raise their arms and welcome the darkness,

palming the blank spaces, touching everything.
Always they return home safely, like blind men
who know it is morning by feeling shadows.

And always they wake up as themselves again.
That's why I want to say something astonishing
like: *Our hearts are leaving our bodies.*

Our hearts are thirsty black handkerchiefs
flying through the trees at night, soaking up
the darkest beams of moonlight, the music

of owls, the motion of wind-torn branches.
And now our hearts are thick black fists
flying back to the glove of our chests.

We have to learn to trust our hearts like that.
We have to learn the desperate faith of sleepwalkers who rise out of their calm beds

and walk through the skin of another life.
We have to drink the stupefying cup of darkness
and wake up to ourselves, nourished and surprised.

III

The last moment of winter begins
With a starling flapping its feathery wings
In the fog like the dingy gray handkerchief
Of an old woman waving good-bye

To a slow train pulling slowly
Out of the last abandoned station
Stationed like a sentinel at the furthest
Outpost of the mountains. It's snowing.

The woman standing on the blurred platform
And the soldier blowing smoke through his chapped hands
Are like the two halves of a single face
Staring down at the steel tracks straightening

Across the broken spine of the country,
The stubble fields, and the thick iron corridors
Narrowing into the narrow side of a mountain.
The fog is thickening with snow and stars

When the last starling flies up like a baton!
And now the wind begins to play, the wind
Is playing its armful of stars and smoke,
The wind is plucking the broken strings

Of the broken branches. And so the
Old woman walking home through the stubble
Fields and the young sentinel pacing off
Down a long wooden corridor of fog

Are part of the same windy song, part
Of the same fistful of blurred notes,
Part of the same broken string proclaiming
Winter is over, now something else begins.

To begin, and to begin again, and to begin with
The operatic beginnings of another winter:
First the shattered light, the shattered wings
Of a dead moth shivering in the tall grass,
The stammering October wind. And then

The pandemonium of dusk, the thunderous
Pandemonium of a dead sun going down
Over the wild regalia of horses and swords
Flashing like stars against the dark poplars.
Already an icy crescent has broken through

The stillness of those branches, already
A sheen of ice covers the thick blanket
Of this grass. Night has risen suddenly
Over the slow earth of Indian summer, this
Rich summer earth. This night. *That moth!*

And then the Cossacks ride through the village
Like winter itself. And when they ride out
There are women moaning on their doorsteps
Like slaughtered cows, there are old men
In skullcaps bellowing in the cold like

Foghorns, or beggars at the wailing wall,
Or naked little children running through the
Streets with their startled black intestines
Flowing in their hands like warm milk.
It's snowing at the city gates. And Babel,

It's that murderous human longing of ours
To be anywhere else, to be someone else,
To speak in the genre of silence, to wear
Spectacles in the blue mist of autumn.
If only we knew what the wind knows:

That snowstorms are winter clarified, that music
Widens in the stillness of this cruelty.

INTERLUDE DURING WAR:
PAUL KLEE

An interminable wrestle with numbers
And here I am, working inside the
Gray bowels and belly of a desk
Thrust up to my elbows in paper
When suddenly, through a cube of light
Swallowing its last handful of dusk
I discover some rare, Italian pigments
Mixed with genius on the window.

Golds and blacks. A metallic yellow
From yesterday's rainstorm, and an oily red twig
Slipping out from a crack in the pavement.
Imagine: the true resourcefulness of mud!
Thus scrawled in charcoal for several hours
Oblongs and square patches of ground,
Constellations over mean houses, and an
Orange balloon on a courtesan's window.

All this I did without warning and without
Irony, until suddenly stopped, surprised
By the thought of Lily's blue ankle
Inside my infantry boot. So I am not
Home after all! But then drew this:
A little black crescent peering out
From its branches well over the rooftops,
Carved like an ankle or

A mouth puckered up in the clouds.
Revolving its small foot or smiling sadly
On the chalky hopes of soldiers. But mostly
It marvels at the storm, at the colorful
Explosions of wind, the earnest red dyes,
The chicken scratchings of rain, and
The enigma of thunder, terrifying the houses
But shaped like wishbones in the sky.

Listen, it only takes a moment
to move, to knot ourselves
together like the ends of a rope
longing to be knotted together,

but let's avoid it, let's wait.
Ropes, even the sturdiest ropes,
pull, they strain, struggle, eventually
they break. But think of it;

in a still life a knife
pauses above a platter of
meat, it only takes a second, and
poof it becomes the idea of a knife,

the drawing of a knife suspended
in the air like a guillotine
about to weightlessly drop on the
neck of a murderer and send him

shrieking into oblivion forever,
but it never happens, the knife
keeps falling and falling, but never
falls. That knife could be us.

The milk on the table is always
about to spill, the meat could be
encased in wax paper to be
protected from flies, but it's

not, it's unnecessary, the flies
threaten to descend on the
exposed meat, but they can't, they're
no longer flies, but a painting of flies,

the blood pooled on the platter
of meat never evaporates, it can't;
look, it's still there; and if I
never touch you, well then, we never die.

Listen, even lovers have still lives,
have whole months when they hang
together like moths on an unlit
light bulb, waiting for the bulb to light,

but if it never does then the moths
survive, meat should be allowed
to sit on the table forever
without being devoured by flies

and if that's not possible, well
then we still have this picture,
the still life not of how it will be,
but of how it was, for the knife and the meat

and the flies, and for us the night we
hesitated together. From now on, love,
we will always be about to destroy
each other, always about to touch.

To begin with a light as vivid and warm
As the strong brown hands of my mother
Braiding my grandmother's hair
For a Saturday night dance in the country.
All over the house there are preparations:
In the basement my grandfather is soaping
His gray beard in a thick mist rising
From the water in a steamy iron tub;
Upstairs my sister is trying on her pink shoes
And red slip, and her red shoes and
Pink slip, and her orange dress. Outside
I am watching my peasant friend Talosha
Trying to teach my eldest brother Claude
A real Polish polka. Father says it is
As hopeless as trying to teach a French pear
Sapling to grow Moroccan apples. Everyone laughs.
Everyone. I'd like to begin with a light
As warm and vivid as that laughter.

And I'd like to end with the red interior
Of an enormous country house blazing with lights
For the dance. My grandfather is wearing
A string tie someone sent him from America,
My grandmother is drinking real peach brandy
In a coffee cup. My mother is dressed
In a dress the color of crushed strawberries
And my sister has decided on a navy skirt
With a red sash and a bright red scarf tied
Around her neck. Even my brother can't take
His eyes off her. And me? Well, I'm drunk.
I am whirling around and around the dance floor
With Talosha until the bright peasant blouses
Become a steady blur circling on the walls,
A dizzy whirling of lights and stars. And then

My father carries me upstairs and puts me
In an enormous double bed with satin sheets.
And then nothing else but sleep. And this:

All night I hear the music in my head;
All my life I dream of dancers whirling
Through the trees like colorful wild beasts.

"It is not enough to have memories.
One must also be able to forget them."

It has taken centuries to discover

The heart is a pomegranate
Blistered with seeds, bruised and swollen
With secrets, too ripe for carving
But not for splitting its seams
Since the rind, too, has its ways
And seasons. My skin is me. We travel

Hard, vanishing inwards, learning
How a red disc that throbs
In a cage of branches can become
An orange bulb lighting a barred window
In a monastery in Odessa, and the
Monastery is really only a prison, and
The orange bulb is a violent lamp working

Inside of me. Showing an obscure thing:
How a monk in a white robe kneels
To the icon of a god he doesn't believe in,
Teaching himself to pray and not
To sing, although there's a voice buried
Somewhere in his ribs, and a pomegranate is
Tattooed to his sleeve. The window is open.
An orange bulb is showing through the trees. We

Are riding on horses with muzzled heads
Into the river, and like the river
We are pushing our sore bodies outwards
Against the skin. Like monks we kneel
On steel floors where we've always been.

Because I believe now that the heart
Is a pomegranate consuming itself
And that even the secrets we disclose
Remain secrets, we deserve a great kindness.
We have wasted nothing, traveling through

Open spaces into ourselves.

The country women speak of ships,
ghostly vessels or great men-of-war
gutting on these rocks, these cliffs,
and always at this time of year

when the staunch harvest moon
swells over the sky of these crops
revolving like a searchlight, or a white balloon
wobbling over the steep, sloping drop

from the sky to the ocean floor.
This is the clearest night of the year,
yet always there's an accident, a flaw;
a slamming of iron, and a crew

going down amongst the dead
shouting at the rocks and fish,
puddling the waves in blood.
The sea sucks color from the flesh

and washes the bodies ashore.
By morning, however, they have disappeared;
the ship has been dragged down by the tide,
and nothing remains for another year.

Nothing to mar our wealth at Equinox
but the country women's story of need;
how the drowned sailors scream for crops
giving earth back to the sea.

I am the voices that fill you with silence,
The door slightly open, like a robe.
You are the teacher brushing my breasts
With your elbow, hearing the soft

Purr of my paintbrush on canvas. Yes,
I am the cat sliding out of reach
Like a moon evading the long arms
Of a tree on the river: You know

I am married. You know I am plotting
A long journey down the Yellow River
In a camel's-hair jacket, alone. Darling,
I am leaving you behind, like a door

Gently closed. You were planning
A vacation to China. No longer. You
Were touching my shoulders with your
Hands. No more. I am the telephone,

You are the wrong number. Or you are
The phone call, no one is home, but
Could Be, or Might Have Been, or Won't.
I am the silence that fills you with voices.

She means nothing to me
Familiar old crone, spoiled Latin bitch
With her rumpled palms and swampy breasts
Fattening nightly, offering herself to strangers.

What does it matter to me
If she bares her bosom to the trees
Like a spayed cat, or an aged whore
Promising a tourist his fortune?

Each day she wastes herself in sleep;
Each night she douses herself in perfume
And buries her body in layers of cloth,
In red petticoats and white slips

Until finally, at the end of each month
She emerges, dancing from the clouds
Naked, leaving her wet clothes
In a puddle of branches!

Let her dance all night if she
Wants to, let her dance on the lake
Or in the folds of the red curtains,
But keep her away from me

With her drowsy lips and warm mouth,
With her tongue pressed against the glass.
Each night I tell myself that she's only
A pomegranate, or at best, the skull of a cabbage,

And yet she continues to haunt me,
To keep me awake with her sensual dancing;
And turning away from the window
I can hear her calling to me

With my voice, nuzzling under my arm,
Singing to me from the moisture of my lungs;
That staggering old bitch, my heart,
Flaming up in a chest of branches!

A WALK WITH VALLEJO
IN PARIS

I am walking down Rue de la Paix on a Wednesday night in late August, a dusty night near the end of the month of Americans, a sad month when all the Parisians have fled south for their holiday, leaving only the tourists, and the shopkeepers, and the Algerians. It is a night when the heat of daylight somehow turns into the heat of midnight without ever passing through the liquids of dusk, a night of anger and nerves, and I am trying to decide where to get something to eat: at the soup kitchen near Place de la République where if I'm lucky and the lines aren't too long I can get a bowl of thin broth and a lecture on God in Arabic, *"le Dieu qui nous aime bien,"* or at the cafeteria of Cité Universitaire where the American students are generous, but where the guards usually chase me away. *"Nous n'avons pas besoin d'un autre Américain sans portefeuille."* We don't need another American without a wallet. So I opt for the relative safety of the Algerian soup line, though on the way I stop a man with a family to ask for money. Sometimes a man will feel generous in front of his wife and children, but this time the woman only clasps her pocketbook and he says, *"Je ne parle pas anglais."* I ask him in French. *"Je n'ai pas d'argent moi,"* he says. "And I don't speak English."

At Place de la République I discover that the thick double line extends around two solid blocks. There are so many Algerians without work in Paris that I won't be able to get inside the building until dawn. I am trying to decide what to do when suddenly I see César Vallejo with his hands thrust into his pockets standing under a street lamp. He nods to me. As I walk over to him I notice that his pants are patched with rags, there are deep holes in his shoes, and a single tear runs from his shoulder through the center of his shirt. He is so thin that I can see the post behind him by staring at his chest. "Come with me," he says. "I know a place where we can get some soup." And then: "I always feel sad for Americans when they're hungry. Everyone is desperate when they're poor, but Americans are pathetic."

We begin to walk and from then on Vallejo is always ahead of me. I have to hurry to stay with him like a small child trying to keep up with his father. Sometimes he stops abruptly to peer at something that interests him on the sidewalk. But where I see a weed he sees a muskrat; where I see a muskrat he sees the face of a woman. This doesn't seem to disturb him. "What matters is that we are both looking down," he says. "When you get lonely enough you'll see the face of a woman too."

While we walk his head is always on the ground, his hands are clenching and unclenching in his pockets. Sometimes he is silent for whole blocks, sometimes he talks to me. "There's a war going on," he says, "and I am always hungry. *J'ai toujours faim. Siempre tengo hambre.* Sometimes I think these are different things, and to tell the truth I am less frightened of hunger than of the Catholics in Spain. They're both murderers but at least hunger rises out of your own belly to strangle you. It doesn't pretend to come from God. Other times I think they are the same."

Finally Vallejo stops in front of a crowded tenement. "You go in," he says, and disappears into a lamp post. "Vallejo!" But he is gone. So I go inside and knock on the first door I can find in the dark hallway. Soon a woman comes to answer. She is very ugly and thin, even thinner than I am, even thinner than Vallejo, though not so tall, and she is wearing a tattered pink housecoat soaked in sweat. When she sees me she begins to weep. She must think I am someone else because she insists she's been waiting for me for so long, she didn't think I'd ever come, thank God I'm finally there, the children have been starving, the landlord has been threatening to throw them into the streets, and the children are so hungry, they haven't eaten in three days. And suddenly I see them behind her, a boy and a girl, tiny and naked, wrapped around their mother's legs, very frightened and excited. They are crying. At first I try to resist but the woman is persistent, she is dragging me into her apartment and soon the children have stopped crying, they are jumping on my lap, the woman is putting her arms around my neck, they are so happy I am there. And I am glad to be there. I hardly recognize myself and soon I am promising them everything: to bring food, to buy clothing, to pay the landlord, to find a job. And it is only later, when the children have gone to sleep and the woman takes off her housecoat that I see in her bruised body the eyes of Vallejo, the hungry eyes of Vallejo, and the sad face of the weeds, and the muskrats, and the war.

IV

LITTLE POLITICAL POEM

after Nazim Hikmet

Tonight I saw so many windows
lit up in so many different houses
each little square of glass
lit up separately, like a flame,

so many flames together, the repetition
of so many lights in so many houses
all lit up separately, but

somehow all flaming together, too,
like a single fire, say, a housewarming,
an entire block blazing with the light
from a single window, so many windows

in so many houses on so many nearly
identical streets in so many different
neighborhoods in so many different cities. . . .

Tonight I saw so many windows
blazing alone, almost blazing together
under a single sky, under so many
different skies all weaving together

through so many different countries. . . .

FACTORIES

for Susan Stewart

Everywhere in New York City there are factories
flinging their broken windows into the streets
raining sawdust and glass crying out with the
soft voices of women whispering Puerto Rican names
whispering my name and wearing their dark shadows
like petticoats and their graffiti like too much makeup
over their scarred bricks their used up bodies

they are always stained they have walls
broken off like the stumps of cripples
I'm sorry but this is how it is with me
everywhere I turn I find the ruined mouths
and damp animals of yes and when
I lie down to sleep at night I hear

dry pistons setting into motion like
galloping horses their hooves are echoing
on concrete their iron hearts are hammering
they are churning like diesels bursting out of
tunnels out of mountains out of factories
and shedding silence like an extra skin
pumping blood through the stillness of my arteries

Come home. I don't want to sound frightened,
but this morning when I got back from work
I couldn't scrub the grease off my hand;

it had settled into my skin like a deep film,
the veins were black, and the barges
were blurred on the flayed rivers in my palm.

The warehouses were empty. The streets were jumbled,
and the canals tunneled out in all directions
none of them homeward, though somehow

they all funneled back into an open basin,
a blank sea, like a tree gathering in
its last branches, or a map smudged with dirt.

I don't want to sound desperate, but all night
I could hear my feet opening narrow graves
in the sawdust, the rats crawling through a maze

of pipes inside my chest; and I spent
so many hours stacking crates inside of crates
inside of crates, like paper cups, so many crates,

so many other places. . . . Come home.
This morning when I pressed my hand to the glass
I saw a black sun buried in sludge

and a thousand rivers clogged with waste
running into the basin of a single map
muddied with features, so many features,

so many faces, but none of them yours.

WALKING THE UPPER
WEST SIDE, WITH LORCA

It begins with the humped bodies of cars
Stalled on the bridge, and the first lights
Booming like drums from New Jersey.

Almost as a thought the moon rises
Out of a gray mist of smokestacks,
Black and blistered like a bruise swelling
Under the broken skin of fog,
A dark nail of light, or the face
Of the one old woman who ushers in
Every morning with a shriek, pounding
The door for cigarettes, calling us Jews.

Today you gave her some new Spanish coins
Muttering the wrong language, and stepped over
Three crippled drunks gaping in the doorway.

Once we're up here on Broadway
Smoke eats away at our eyes, it is
The rhythm of so many different bodies
All going somewhere in the night, some
Of us going anywhere. It is the
Voice of two eternal students selling
Ragged pamphlets on the street, the sound
Of one young woman in a torn dress

Moaning for Christ on the corner
While the subways moan underfoot. Nearby
a woman smiles under a street lamp, half

Of her face torn away by shadows.
Everything is coming at us in English
But when we cross over at Amsterdam
Zigzagging past the tenements, suddenly
A starling begins singing to us
His pure Spanish lyrics, crying out
That he is homesick, like you. And all
Night he follows us through the streets

Calling out from the windows, crying out
From the doorsteps, from the three staggering
Trees staggered on the sidewalk. And soon

You begin singing back at him
Your deep Gypsy howl from the streets,
The booming lights of New Jersey, the dead moon
Fractured in the smokestacks, the sidewalk
Legacy of beggars, the night swallowed up
By voices in the fog, the rumble of
These subways in this city, the poetry
That matters, the loneliness of America.

A TRUE ACCOUNT
OF THE FABULOUS ASCENT
OF A UNICORN WITH
A RETARDED GIRL IN
NEW YORK CITY LAST NIGHT

"The whole traditionary character of the unicorn
as the antagonist . . . of the lion."
—De Quincey

"The Unicorne, whose horne is worth halfe a City."
—Dekker

It was as if she had always been waiting
but without knowing it, like a heart
in the chest of a dead saint,
or a clock that had never once been set.

Imagine a lamp extinguished in the rain
and never relit, or a girl walking out of her body.

Often she would claim there were voices
flapping around in her nightshirt, like moths
searching for a single wick in the unlit
oven of her chest. And perhaps,

like a target, she was right.

Everywhere in her body there were doors
that had never been opened, rooms
that were stifling hot, and walls tipped
over on their sides, like floors. Butterflies
threw themselves outwards in her lungs
but the sky was a plaster ceiling and
their limp bodies fell backwards in the mud.

Not that it mattered much to her, of course:
a young girl smothering her face in a pillow.

But one night she felt a summer wind
nuzzling under her skirt like the warm nose
of a horse nudging her for sugar, or
a wild dog sticking its paw

through an iron cage. Later, she slept
and dreamt of a steel lock clicking shut
around her waist, and a dozen wings crumpling
on her legs. And when she awoke
there was a strange horse
laying a golden spike across her lap

like a new rifle, dazzling her
with the brightest colors she had ever seen.

She could already hear the panting in his side
and the deep pounding in his chest
after a long run, and she was not afraid.
She even imagined that he was lonely
and she could already feel her hands
roving across his face.

                She did not know,
of course, that he had once been extinct
or that he had traveled across several centuries
of desert that very night. She only knew
that he was there now for her as a lover
and after a little while she could
no longer really tell if it was
her palms or his neck that was sweating.
And she didn't care, either.

And that was how New Yorkers looked up last night
and marveled at an ancient artery of stars
shining through the smog, and a solitary
wing rising from the river
like a girl bending over a strange horse.
And somehow it

was almost as if they had always been waiting
for that single blaze of light
scrawled like a wish over the entire city.

DENIAL

We don't want a coffin nailed shut
but the sex we deny to ourselves
keeps both of us hammering in the dark
like a naked widow trying to fix the house
while her husband falls through space,
or two cars converging in a tunnel.
So this is the meaning of loneliness:
your body closed up like a factory
without workers, or a hospital without beds.

And now I'm talking about building.
So what if that means a house
without bricks, or a pool without water?
And who ever needed fish for fishing?
I'm talking sense. When I tap your back
the spike in my hands can become
a drill in your legs. And watch:
I'm taking the mirrors from my chest
and installing a door with windows.

Please don't call it a ladder of circles
driven by a broken wind from the sea.
Yes, I know the wind scrapes at the wheel
all night long, and that the waves claw at the ships,
and that the tide under our feet is relentless.
I know you know the true motion of stillness

but don't we descend into that stillness
only to rise again? Because it is not the wheel
but the viciousness of turning, the relentless
climb into the sky climbing in circles
like squirrels quarreling in a feeder, or ships
leaving the dock but never setting out to sea

that disturbs and compels us. It is not the sea
with its quarries of weeds and its quarrelsome ships
roaring as it pleases into the stillness
of its own blank voice, its own relentless
weaving and unweaving a confusing surface of circles,
a tiresome system of echoes. A buzzard that wheels

past the shimmering wood of the ferris wheel
frightens us into a momentary silence; its relentless
wings slice and flatten as it hovers in circles
over a shallow wreckage swinging in the sea
while we continue moving into our own stillness
first toward and then away from the stunned ship

now quartered under the surf. The ship
we ride in is a cage of steel circles
encircled by the fleck and moaning of the sea.
We try to speak, but the stillness
is deafening, words fall behind us, and the wheel
lifts into the sky. Besides, the sea is a relentless

mother, and like the wind she seems to relent less
and less as the night wears into a deeper stillness.
We watch the buzzard revolving over the ruined ship
like a descending plane or a horizontal wheel
rotating toward the kill. And still the sea
keeps turning and turning in a nightmare of blank circles.

We descend. The wheel continues its stupid circle
into the sky, but we are moving into a new stillness
relentless as the black ships setting out to sea.

Perhaps it begins in silence, silence and awe.
Because think of the way, as a child, you could stand
Under the stars, dry and leafless in the open tent
Thinking of nothing, I mean not thinking of anything
Because there was nothing to think about, knowing that soon
The acrobat would lean out of his marvelous skin
And throw himself into the empty spaces,
Letting the wind gnaw gently at his limbs
Tortured into new postures, exotic faraway places .
But not anticipating or even expecting it yet
Because it was better to let it come at you
Suddenly, like a cold shock of winter rain, or
The black wing of a storm, the crowd's insanity!
How you despised the clowns with their clumsy vigilance
And warped, colorful faces, their mockingbird smiles,
Although you already knew that they, too, were
Part of the meaning, part of the circumstance, and
That being there under the booming lights and veined sky
Was enough, maybe it was even what you could expect,
Like those pale green sunsets marred by oil derricks.
It was enough. And it could not be changed.

Once, when I was still only an apprentice
I spilled out of an iron swing into some hay
And suddenly remembered watching hundreds of ducks
Startled out of a wintry, New Hampshire pond
By a solitary old man wearing a fur hat and
Carrying a hunting rifle. Afterwards I discovered
That the rusty swing was faulty and that although
No one admitted to being present, the ringmaster's rifle
Had exploded in a tent near the back of a stream
Just as I was falling out of my double somersault.
And this proved that I had relived the experience

Almost exactly, and that the mind is really a beacon
Or else a chipmunk scurrying around on its wheel,
Where we keep going away from ourselves,
Going away and returning.

                    Now it's autumn.
The leaves are coming off the branches
In a solemn procession of oranges and bright reds,
Dim purples, and even a few speckled, late summer greens.
And you can still remember standing in the momentary dark
Watching his right foot curl casually over the rope
And then his other foot swung up like a rider
Into a stirrup, and then the long vertical climb
High into the lights. Where the platform was a
Sand dune, or a lighthouse, and the crowd
Was a watery blur, a colorful syrup of streamers
You despised. And then the spotlight began rising
Like the beacon, the wooden platform evaporated,
And he finally moved. Yes, you can still remember
How some were repelled and turned away; some thought
This was a spectacle and mistook his small, tattooed body
For a zoo animal; some actually started to tremble,
And a few began their long, disfiguring applause.
But for you he was always and only a man
Spreading out like wings against the dark canvas,
Squeezing in and out of his own body into reservoirs
Of awed silence. A man rippling above us like the wind.
But then it was over. There was clapping, perhaps an ovation
And his body was closer, bunched up like an insect's.
It no longer mattered, but you hated him then, hated
His muscular scraping against the floor. His smallness.
You hated him. And you wished you were dead.

But then it began in earnest, like October.
And it didn't take very long to discover
That the body is a child, or even a house pet
And that house pets need to be trained; children
Aren't born to listen; they have to be taught.
And so you learned to twist in and out of yourself
Like a blanket hung up to dry, and you learned
To wait, to carve your body into empty spaces.
This training had to be done with real seriousness
Like living, like a chipmunk going around and around
In his cage, or a ferris wheel that keeps going up and up and
Even further up, and then slides weightlessly down.
And you began to understand that the ferris wheel
Is revolving inside of us, and that even chipmunks
Have dignity. Dignity and great courage. But then
One night someone clapped at the wrong moment, loudly,
Like a rifle going accidentally off, and this
Hurt you very much, you thought back to the ducks,
Though somehow you managed to steady yourself
In the dark; you still didn't fall into the stands.

For years you thought of the ugliness of that applause
And of the endless monotony of your small, turning wheel,
But then one morning it begins to bloom inside of you
Almost casually, as offhanded as an opinion
Although, like an opinion, it gets steadier and steadier,
Like a drunk it eventually begins to sober,
Nurturing on itself as a seed tossed carelessly
Into an iron pot in an abandoned greenhouse in winter
Only to peek out years later from its colorless vine
As a rose; a scrawny, pink, purplish, ugly, little
Short-stemmed rose blossoming inside of you.
And suddenly you realize: This is hell. And it *is*.
It really is. And then you think: I have already
Lived through it. And perhaps that's true also.

And then you discover that it doesn't even matter.
And this is amazing. Because you still
Have to go on dangling over the starless nets and
Under the nets of stars, climbing over dazed watery crowds
With your chipmunk's passion for movement, for circles.
And now whenever someone is repelled by your body
You think of the unspeakable reservoirs in the mind,
The silt, and the way a lake can continue rippling
Long after the last pebbles have finally disappeared.
Or how a vacancy rises up to surround the violent shock
Of a single rifle fired once on a pond in early winter.
Look, the ducks are sliding away from us toward the stars
Although the stars, millions of miles beyond, are already dead.
Sometimes when you stare up into their black, leafless vines
You can feel the awe, the silence and the awe,
And the wind flapping against ropes and canvas sides.
Because you know now that whenever you move
There are whole centuries moving behind you.
Fossils cradle in your bones. The deepest oceans
Rise in your bird blood, yes, and you can already
Feel the distance in your lungs, the distance, and
The stillness spreading its blank wings inside you.

This is a song for the speechless,
the dumb, the mute and the motley,
the unmourned! This is a song for every
pig that was too thin to be slaughtered
last night, but was slaughtered
anyway, every worm that was hooked
on a hook that it didn't expect,
every chair in New York City that has
no arms or legs, and can't speak English,
every sofa that has ever been torn
apart by the children or the dog
and earmarked for the dump, every sheet
that was lost in the laundry, every
car that has been stripped down and
abandoned, too poor to be towed away,
too weak and humble to protest.
Listen, this song is for you even if
you can't listen to it, or join in;
even if you don't have lungs, even
if you don't know what a song is,
or want to know. This song is for
everyone who is not listening tonight
and refuses to sing. Not singing
is also an act of devotion; those
who have no voices have one tongue.

V

"Taedet coeli convexa tueri."
　　　　　　　　—Virgil (*Aeneid* IV 451)

"Dark is the sun, and loathsome is the day."
　　　　　　　　—Samuel Johnson

SONATA

for Janet

Wake up and listen, tonight
the dark wind trembles in the pines
like the nervous hands of a young girl

playing a sonata for her grandmother
for the first time, or like
the spindly legs of an old woman

walking home through a field of stumped
elms buried in the fog. The girl
hits the wrong note, just once, and

suddenly the old woman begins to hum,
loudly and out of tune, a cradle song
to ward off the darkest shadows.

Wake up! And wake my mother
in her bed and your mother in her bed,
my grandmother in her coffin. Wake up

our daughters and granddaughters still unborn.
Tonight the wind is playing the same song
over and over again, the same sonata,

yes, with the same wrong note
relentless as time, unbearable and human.

Sometimes I think that my body is a vase
With me in it, a blue-tiled Chinese vase

That I return to, sometimes, in the rain.
It's raining hard, but inside the little china vase

There is clean white water circling slowly
Through the shadows like a flock of yellow geese

Circling over a small lake, or like the lake itself
Ruffled with wind and geese in a light rain

That is not dirty, or stained, or even ruffled by
The medley of motors and oars and sometimes even sails

That are washed each summer to her knees. It's raining
In the deep poplars and in the stand of gray pines;

It's snowing in the mountains, in the Urals, in the
Wastes of Russia that have edged off into China;

The rain has turned to sleet and the sleet
Has turned to snow in the sullen black clouds

That have surfaced in the cracks of that Chinese
Vase, in the wrinkles that have widened like rivers

In that vase of china. It's snowing harder and harder
Now over the mountains, but inside the mountains

There is a sunlit cave, a small cave, perhaps,
Like a monk's cell, or like a small pond

With geese and with clear mountain water inside.
Sometimes I think that I come back to my body

The way a penitent or a pilgrim or a poet
Or a whore or a murderer or a very young girl

Comes for the first time to a holy place
To kneel down, to forget the impossible weight

Of being human, to drink clear water.

Smoke blooms like breath from the chimneys
Of the iron boxes pulling into the station
Daily at St. Lazare. These rectangles
Of black screened by a heavy, metallic gray
Are like giant insects dragging themselves forward
On silver tracks; and these tiny squiggles moving
Slowly over the page in indigos and bright pinks
Are like a thousand Parisian citizens pouring out
Of their boxes in a thick waterfall of light,
Or in a crowd of colors mixing on the eye
As on a painter's palette. Think of the way
That colors print and spangle on a young girl's
Summer dress as she rolls in the wet grass
In the garden, or that a steamy landscape of
Flowers blurs and fogs in the morning rain.
I see these colors everywhere and every place
And at all hours of the day and night.

There is only light and its permutations:
Even the flesh is light, even the shadows of
Mice in the corner, or the impression of a
Woman's body lying down on a mattress to rest.
The first thing I see in the morning is light
Steaming through the blank windows like clouds
Of smoke blooming in the fat stacks of chimneys,
And the last thing I see before sleep is a slice of
Purple wedged under my lids before the hard, blunt coins
Of blackness press down on my eyes for the night.
My wife Camille is sick and, perhaps, dying.
Yesterday—with a strange, fascinated horror—I watched
Myself watching the deep grays and yellow golds
Seeping into the hard planes of her face. We have
Never had enough to eat—never—and her lips
Were already turning blue, like a gasping fish.
Hear my words carefully:

I was only interested in the colors of her face!
And I knew then that there was no escape; there is only
This light for me in the unlit world of men.

THE RIVER MERCHANT: A LETTER HOME

Sometimes the world seems so large,
You have no idea. Out here at dusk
The barges pull the heaviest cargo, sometimes
They drag whole ships to the sea. Imagine
The sound of geese shrieking everywhere,
More geese than you can imagine,
Clustered together and flapping like stars.
Sometimes there are two moons shining at
Once, one clouded in the treetops, one
Breaking into shadows on the river.
I don't know what this means.

But from the hill's brow I can see
The lights in every village flickering on,
One by one, but slowly, like this,
Until the whole world gleams
Like small coins. Believe me:
There are so many villages like ours,
So many lights all gleaming together
But all separate too, like those moons.
It is too much. I am older now.
I want to return to that fateful place
Where the river narrows toward home.

This morning it is
The sky hanging behind the river
Like a mottled sheet, a coarse
Blue shirt spangled with pears.
It is the obvious crescent of my own face
Fading on the glass, the steam

From my mouth, steam
From a slow tugboat tugged slowly
Through the iron petals of a bridge
Opening and, yes, clanging shut. It is
A nameless wound swelling under my tongue,
The soft wings beating in my chest, and
The last pigeons breaking out of the water
Like a flurry of snowflakes and fists.

On the other side of the bridge
There is a boy banking a small fire
Of twigs, warming his hands on the flame,
And watching a thin vein of smoke
Merging with a light mist from the river,
A crescent of steam, and a final patch of moon
Faltering in a thicket of chimneys. He has
So many thoughts, so many other secrets
Entangled in that artery of smoke
Scrawled across the wind like a signature.

And so it begins again
Here and now, like this, in our world.
Because it *is* our world, because
The veils are lifting from our windows
And the other faces appear, looking out
At our life together, our new day starting up
With the light from a small fire
Rising into a sky of fists and stars.

I. PROEM: EARLY MORNING

There's an owl who believes in sleep
Still singing in the marsh. Too old
To sing to us, I think, he sings
About old passions: what it means
To keep vigil over the trees, to
Watch the darkness blistering into dark,
To hear the blind fish
Burning through the stream, face up,
Facing the treetops with their eyes.

Age old, he remembers
Animals that are now extinct,
Fish swimming out of their bones
And becoming birds, birds that have blossomed
Into trees. And now he limps
Out of his branches to become that
Old sea hawk, the sun, defeated nightly
But returned to refute the marsh
Rising into the sky on bandaged wings.

II. PARABLE OF WYVERNS

for Trevor Parssinen

It's clear that we imagine these animals
Because we need to, because these animals
In their robust way, need to be imagined,
Need us to imagine them, though it's clear
That, in their own way, they also imagine us.

And so a two-legged beast with a tail
Flared like a peacock's, though, strictly speaking,
Not a peacock's, is flying across
The hot sands of an invisible desert;
A desert that doesn't exist, though it has

Real sands, real mirages with live Arabs, and
Camels that drink water from a trough for horses.
And if you understand the necessity of that trough
Then you will also understand this poem
Which I've chunked on the table like a can

Of coins, with its rattling voice and its parable
Of a country that is still unmapped, although
Others have explored its strange terrain:
A fabulous country south of the mind
Where camels are horses and wyverns fly.

III. CANTATA FOR A DUTCH ELM

The suburban tree rustles like sheets of paper:
It knows it will be cut down. The birds
In that tree have already abandoned their nests
Though they've delayed going south for the winter.
They're sad, and it's a long trip for the young.

The wind that knifes through the branches
Could almost be a surgeon cutting the heart
From the lungs of his patient, and spilling
Blood on the table, though the table could also
Be a mattress, since worms bed down in the mud.

When it starts to rain the birds
Wheel through the air, nostalgic for home:
And soon the branches begin to tear
With pride, trying to resist the wind.
It would be so much easier simply to die!

And far away in the city the secretaries
Are rushing for shelter; businessmen
Are holding up raincoats and newspapers;
Housewives are hurrying to their station wagons.
And slowly the drowned weeds begin to float on the pavement.

Rainwater swells with blood in the sewers.

IV. DUSK: ELEGY FOR THE DARK SUN

A sword is bandaged in the clouds.
Call it the sun, though others
May think it's an anchor
Sunk in the sky, or a knife
Carved into the leaves.
But call it the sun. And call
The hands pressed to its face
The clouds, though others may think
They're a blanket containing heat
Or four shoes clapped onto a horse.
That horse can run. And call the field
Where it runs the sky, and the stable
Where it rests the sea. And the hay
That it eats is blue and yellow.
Call it the rain and the wind.
These imaginings make it possible
To survive, to endure the hard light,
Though darkness is floating in.
And that thing breaking in my chest
Is more than a heart; it is also
The sun bandaged in a sheath of clouds
And thrown up over the waves
Like a lifebuoy, like a hand
Trying to call its fellow men.

TRANSFIGURED NIGHT,
COME DOWN TO ME, SLOWLY

I am walking through the cemetery one more time
waiting for the night-blooming cereus to bloom
once more, on its own, in the dark. I am
listening to the serious wind ruffle the broad
chest of grass, the tired muscles of earth,
the scrawny roots that reach into the mud
like a blistered foot, or a bony hand.
I am watching a cluster of green fists shine
on the bough of a pear tree like enormous
gray moths, or a string of tiny lamps.

Transfigured night, come down to me, slowly.
Bring me your wind and your stars, bring me
a yellow wing brushed against my eyes,
a clear window of moonlight that shatters
once more, on its own, yes, in the dark.
By now the old griefs have hardened
in my chest like a thick chunk of fat.
By now my hands have swollen into fists.
I want to hear the dead lips moving.
I want to feel the thumbprint of another life.

A NOTE ABOUT THE AUTHOR

Edward Hirsch was born in Chicago, Illinois, in 1950 and educated at Grinnell College and the University of Pennsylvania. His poems have appeared in a large number of magazines and periodicals—among them *Poetry, The Nation, The New Republic, Partisan Review, The New Yorker,* and *Georgia Review.* He has received several awards from the Academy of American Poets and was awarded an Amy Lowell Traveling Fellowship for 1978–79.

A NOTE ON THE TYPE

This book was set on the Linotype in Granjon, a type named in compliment to Robert Granjon, type cutter and printer in Antwerp, Lyons, Rome, Paris. Granjon, the boldest and most original designer of his time, was one of the first to practice the trade of type founder apart from that of printer.

Linotype Granjon was designed by George W. Jones, who based his drawings on a face used by Claude Garamond (1510–1561) in his beautiful French books. Granjon more closely resembles Garamond's own type than do any of the various modern faces that bear his name.

Composed, printed, and bound by American Book–Stratford Press, Inc., Brattleboro, Vermont, and Saddle Brook, New Jersey

Designed by Albert Chiang